Colors Collected

COLORS
COLLECTED

**Poetry Inspired By The
Hues Of Life**

Celaine Charles

Palmetto Publishing Group
Charleston, SC

Colors Collected
Copyright © 2019 by Celaine Charles
All rights reserved

Cover design by Anna Vowels
First Edition

Printed in the United States

ISBN-13: 978-1-64111-446-2
ISBN-10: 1-64111-446-0

Dedicated to my family ~

To my husband for being the blue in my sky, giving me free reign to write when the moments called. For my eldest daughter's eyes of hope, sending pictures of sights she knew full well I needed to see, and supporting me from every viewpoint. For my younger daughter's belief in the artist inside my soul, filling in the gaps when I needed it. And for my son's ability to stretch out of car windows to capture the sun's rays at just the right angle, so I could write about them.

You are all my rainbow.

Acknowledgements

My gratitude to the journals below for publishing and/or honoring my original pieces:

Channillo: All color poems, pages 1–45
The Sunlight Press: "White Blossoms," page 51
Nine Muses Poetry: "The Color of Love," page 53
Pacific Northwest Writer's Association, Literary Contest, 2017:
  "Songs of Timeless Lore," page 2
  "Time Home," page 11

Citation for "No Blue to Drown in," page 13:
  MacDonald, Fiona. *There's Evidence Humans Didn't
  Actually See Blue Until Modern Times,* Science Alert,
  7 Apr. 2018, www.sciencealert.com/humans-didn-
  t-even-see-the-colour-blue-until-modern-times-
  evidence-suggests. Accessed 2 June 2018.

Table of Contents

1. Green   1
2. Songs of Timeless Lore   2
3. The Violas Give You Away   3
4. My Father   5
5. Shadows   6
6. Hopeful Insomnia   7
7. Rejection   8
8. Victory Cries   10
9. Time Home   11
10. Time is Pale Yellow   12
11. No Blue to Drown in   13
12. Fire and Chocolate   15
13. Patience   17
14. These Daffodils   18
15. The Bees Know   20
16. Dandelion   22
17. Black Raven Eats the Sun   23
18. Wise Owl Waits   25
19. Inchworm Frets   27
20. Black of Night   29
21. Colors   31
22. That Pine   32
23. Native Time Travel   35
24. I Live in the Rain   37
25. Forest, Golden Brown   38
26. Mango Moon   40
27. Shades of Sorrow   41

28. Poinsettia   42

29. The Edge of Aging   44

30. Earth's Honesty   45

31. Stitching Left Behind   47

32. Gossamer Soul   48

33. These Hills (of Coastal Oregon)   49

34. Homecoming   50

35. White Blossoms   51

36. The Color of Love   53

37. About the Author   55

Dear Treasured Reader,

I am thrilled to share my book of poetry with you. Inside you will find a handful of poems collected from my poetry series, Colors (Channillo. com), as well as new pieces available only in this book.

Why colors? As I walk through life, colors speak to me in hues of joy and sorrow, victory and fear. Whether zealous or thoughtful, their meanings ring true. They stay with me until I preserve them on a page. From the striking red breast of a robin, to the darkest shadow behind the sun; the world has a lot to say when I slow down and listen.

For my series on Channillo, I challenged myself to publish two new poems twice a week for six months, completing my series at sixty-two poems. In December 2018, Colors was nominated for three awards and won all three awards: Best Poetry Series, Best New Series, Best Continuing Series. I am forever grateful to my readers.

All proceeds from my Channillo series online are donated to Mary's Place, a Seattle-based organization helping children and families facing homelessness. Although my series is now complete, it is still live and earning money for this establishment. Please consider joining Channillo and following me as an author to keep funds flowing to Mary's Place through Channillo for Charities. A bonus in subscribing to Channillo is discovering new authors in various genres. There's something for everyone.

Thank you for supporting me as an artist. I must also give grace to above for the inspiration and motivation in completing this endeavor. I hope to continue growing as a writer and am grateful for the opportunity to share my work. May these poems find meaning in your hearts.

Celaine Charles

Green

Colors come alive as my father drives
along curves and bends on old
forgotten roads.

Trees push past with urgency,
stitch their hues together,
almost one,

almost hemlock, almost pine,
douglas, cedar, spruce,
chroma blurs,

swelling as one flame,
alive and pulsing
like fire

crackles behind wooded pyres.
Flames lick the sky,
scarlet red,

its heat pulls to embrace,
to be something more in my soul
than just itself;

there is no other name for green.

Songs of Timeless Lore

Words come with the rain
while sunlight
fades
   any flow of language.

Muddled meanings swell
in pools of
drips
   dropped in hopeful fluke.

Phrases unborn, desire
true heartbeats,
stream
   like silver threads of verse.

Bursting like tiny bombs,
embedded pings
rouse
   aimless addled thoughts

softly, in its goad
to wake, to
write
   songs of timeless lore.

The Violas Give You Away

The violas give you away,
it doesn't matter where you are.
They flutter their violet greetings,
and smack my lips in lemony kisses.

Self-conscious, I peer
behind my shoulder,
eyes shifting side to side, in case
you've really come this time.

It's okay when I don't see you,
because you tickle my back
with your long fingernails,
circle–circle–scratch, circle–circle…

The breeze picks up the petals now,
little lions yawn in lazy summer.
I yawn too, wishing I could awaken
all those years back with you.

Iced tea on the front porch, blue
like the sky, painting horizons
big enough to fall into, roll around,
and pitch white fluffy tents.

Rooster crows to say goodnight,
indifferent with the time of day.

Violas spill out of horse troughs,
just in time for salutations…

unforgotten.

My Father

My father wasn't my father,
but my father he became…

Like a sunset melting sky
bleeding over mountain top
with violet hands grasping,
and apricot eyes glaring,
challenging Night to pry
his fingers from
the hope
he had

in me.

Shadows

Shadows are surprisingly full
of colors, remarkable;
tawny velvet rabbits
blend behind the reeds,
and golden ants, so small,
reflect the sun beneath
protection in the soil,
similar in shade to
the little brown bat
awaiting dusk, the lightest
of shadow shades.

Rich and sable,
shadows are the accent
of the natural world;
in between the yin to the yang,
the black to the white,
always concealing
clandestine secrets,
and treasures mislaid.
The *unfound* wishing
to stay small
in a vast bright world.

Hopeful Insomnia

I get up for a drink of water,
exhaustedly counting the hours
left for me to sleep, to wake,
to return to the same day I've lived
already, several times yesterday,
and the day before.

But hopeful still, this day will be
different. This day will be the one
tossing monotonous to the wind,
rolling down the river of routine,
to the very day I've dreamed about,
the day I've worked to find. Time

has eluded this moment, camouflaged
its essence in childish dreams,
lost goals, challenges, and obstacles,
though still I stand, chin up, facing dawn
while it taunts me, sleepless but wanting,
fearful, yet prickling every sense

beneath my skin, pink and flushed—
Anticipation; because what if today is
the day? So, I count the hours left
for me to sleep, to wake, to return
to bed; counting sheep, horses, and cattle,
for a new day awaits, and what if...

Rejection

The letter came at midday,
when the sky was the same color
as the amber fires
striking havoc
in the center of the state.

Hazy storm clouds with golden seams,
middle-yellow-red,
draped whatever summer day
originated
that morning.

A dispirited sign
of what was to come
from a legal sized envelope,
my own handwriting
on the front,

in hopeful script,
now mournful calligraphy,
bereaving encouragement
to move on,
and so, I am;

neutral.
Pain buried under apathy,
indifference

as a protective layer.
"It just wasn't the right time."

"The wrong fit helps no one."
No passion
blooms from a sky
choked
with smoky stars.

Victory Cries

Victory cries on lofty emerald fields
in grunts and battle calls,
low to the ground,
just under the line.
Colored poppies in formation
until
the wind cracks—

Petals fall as sturdy stalks collide.
And like a wolf's song
carries for miles and miles,
swift and clear in intention,
the pack ascends
as one
to claim tribute.

Time Home

Horses thunder across lands, behind eyelids.
romanticizing what could be
in that place
I'd call home.

It's perfect there, tucked away
in thoughtful corners.
An escape in the night,
scarce moments at a traffic light.

Strictly adamant; red hues call halt,
time ticks, demanding notice
of every tock, rumbling
beneath my skin.

In that moment the horses come
trampling away cares
in dusty billows,
a small gift.

Tiny traces of hope freshen my soul
each time I accept
and reciprocate spending
time home.

Time is Pale Yellow

Time is pale yellow,
like sweetness slips through
honeycomb.
All things good
never lasting
long.

Time moves quick—
s l o w.
Its song changes tempo
after each bridge,
and resting for a breath
can cost you.

Credits roll
as the sun sets.
Vista fades to night,
until the rooster crows,
scene changes,
once again—

Golden promises
awaken with tea
and sweet honey,
like a memory, long
lost to remember
in time gone by.

No Blue to Drown in

Is the blue sky always blue?
Do the Himba notice it as anything other than light?
There is no name for blue in their language,
so, there is no blue sky,
although
the sky is always there.

Blue wasn't founded
in our historical language; the word did not exist.
Then is it really there? And if so, could the feelings
connected with blue
be equally unnatural?
I wish…if it were possible

sadness could be an illusion.
Something we feel only because we've been given
the word. A name to identify it as separate, though,
if it didn't exist,
would salty tears just roll
along chins,

like the sun warms faces, and grass smells
of long summer afternoons?
Without the color blue,
Homer described the ocean as wine dark.

Could depression, deep and red,
simply float away…

because its blue wasn't there
to drown in?

Fire and Chocolate

The fire blazes behind black iron bars,
crackling a song from my youth,
one where warmth coated every inch of my flesh
with marshmallows and chocolate…
chocolate.

Sometimes they give chocolate out at the shelter,
on special occasions,
certainly not on the corner.
Chocolate's a childhood for adults who make their way,
away from this place.

I wonder now in the heat of the flame,
its quilt of amber yellow, bound with bitter-sweetness,
where my way once was,
in my journey long ago,
before I turned that bend…

The one that led me here in the dark night,
with silverware in my pocket,
because it was grandmother's.
And though it's not a complete set, and scratched some,
I have every spoon.

I would never trade them for chocolate,
holding radiance from the bonfire

against my flesh. Here in the trees where I sleep,
the fire crackles songs about childhood,
lulling me on my way.

Patience

Patience is burnt orange;
decalescent
until it fades
bittersweet.

An iron in the fire,
ardent
until the acid bath
cools, making it

malleable.

These Daffodils

It's been done before,
plenty of times,
poets writing verse about daffodils.

But not these daffodils,
not from this place,
where they lay hidden beneath the pine.

Suspended, almost an afterthought,
or accidental at most,
their perfect viewpoint disguised.

I almost didn't see them,
had man not breached this spot,
to spill, encroach, and invade.

And moments pass, keeping
confident yellow secrets
from constantly seeking, unsatisfied eyes.

Resting on a whisper,
hopeful in God's sun,
warmth shading their every effort of un-detection.

Spring tempts me now,
my vision stretched,
falling farther out my window to see—

Four secret daffodils,
standing unsuspectingly
under the pine.

The Bees Know

The bees know;
fly to the brightest shades of magenta
if the grass is green.

Swarm to the fountains of fuchsia,
if the sky behind is blue,
because the bees know

it's in the contrast.
They see the patterns,
venations like a roadmap

to their sweet nectar prize.
But I wonder, though they see
the signs, and they know

where they *should* go,
they are distracted
by the juxtaposition.

Color against color,
Sparkle above shine,
pleasure before duty.

They frolic obligations,
find excuses so bright
they match the sun—

I believe the bees know
how to celebrate
each day luminously.

Dandelion

Oh Dandelion,
I always knew you were a flower;
golden petals like the sun.

You deserve your spot in the garden,
so grow.
Stretch your leaves and reach your roots,

far into the earth's soil   as night shades into day,
deep as the stars   are sunk in the sky,
wide like the river's mouth   hungers for salty seas,

turn your face into the light
and breathe in the space
you belong.

Black Raven Eats the Sun

Black raven,
tired of the day,
used his beak to crack—
to break the surface
of setting sun.

He took a bite
from ticking time
with no remorse,
ripped and tore its flesh,
tongue thrusting.

Threw his head back,
swallowed every bite,
savored every minute
passing down
his esophagus—

Filled his crop
for contemplation
later, as for today
he'd seen enough
human cruelty.

Colorful land
once glowing rich
And savory sweet

Now wastes
Away

Greed and deceit
leave their bitter taste—
Perhaps in time
Raven reconsiders;
rebirths the light.

Wise Owl Waits

Wise owl waits,
watches
tree-scape no longer cedar,
pine, or fir.
Hollow space where once
deer cooled
in gentle shade,
have left the squirrels
wanting.

Owl's vision,
exceptional,
binocular in low light
and knowing
more than man
could surely know,
for if he knew
he would sweep
back below the hillside.

Away-away
the crows would call,
darkly sinister,
reckoning civilization
sinful.
Tsk-tsk building towers
and concrete worlds,

blind patterns now stretch
beneath starlight.

Its glow a curse
to night's hue,
to the natural sense
of wonder,
once alive and thriving
in the trunks of evergreens,
stories never to be told
in lullabies…

though wise owl knew.

Inchworm Frets

Do you think the inchworm frets
the loss of green?
Does he fear his reflection
within silver drops of dew
could be gone,
leaving behind
only pale remnants of hue?

If I write these words, will they
be remembered?
Will children one day find
a poem about a tree,
and wonder
at the vibrant color
described in a verdant forest glen?

What can they hope to gain?
These restless leaders
in our ashen world today—
communication
in a blink,
before inchworm loops
his next step.

But nowhere in our future
can we find color
more concentrated

than the dark stains of politics,
the gun-metal gray
of technology,
and loss.

I know not what the geometrid
yearns for, and perhaps he can blend in
without the green of a tree.
Maybe one day, without classification
for the word, the absence of color
will fade from memory,
no longer needed—

and he will soar into a vast grim sky.

Black of Night

Night Bird takes flight,
hungry to soar
the winds above treetops,
now settled for bed.

Lamp posts glow,
although dimly lit,
still shine sugary
beneath silver stars.

And she waits…
beckoning prey,
a magnet to the small
who flutter.

The gullible ones,
rich and delicious
because they believe
there's more to the light.

She never grants thought
to superstitious worship.
Respect to the dark
demands logistics

and efficiency within
limitations of twilight.

Before the black of night,
she soars...elevated

in knowledge and skill,
as echolocation
bids ease in plucking
the mindless from their beds.

Colors

Colors come in tints;
primarily sky,
golden sun,
and fall-crisp gala.

Shaded by night
under stars,
incandescent,
until light finds way

between gaps,
fallen logs, and leaves
not quite decomposed,
only collected in quietude.

Morning light
stretches
through ivory lace.
Delicate painted branches

create patterns
to stories; old
blended generations
in hues of heritage.

That Pine

My life lived on branches
in that pine
on Cambridge,
now torn down
with the willows in the backyard—
the one that hid my angst,
my tantrums,
my fear.

And you listened that day.
I didn't get the haircut
I didn't want.

And I wore that blue sweater
in July.

And I grew taller
climbing down
my tender childhood.

And like leaves
blowing
in October winds,
my hair ribbons loosened
and fell.
With each one

a memory
gone,
replaced with
responsibility.

And I was gone—
to be you.

My first place on
Alexandria,

with a mattress
on the floor,
and a tea kettle,
red,
from you,
on my stove.

All on my own.

Until
I forgot
to check the oil,
in my car,
now stranded.

And when my babies came,
on Buckeye,

I planted flowers,
orange and gold.
I pulled my own weeds.
For that's what grownups do
when playing house
and planting roots.

And soon, time
blew all my memories bare.
I couldn't quite recall
that pine
standing stoic
out my window,
all those years ago—

Now a guest room
in your house
that holds my heart.

Native Time Travel

When I stand back
against the trunk of an old
douglas, and look up,
the blue patches of sky
shoot out
like slick tunnels through time.

Did I imagine
the smoky current—sweep under
my tipped toes, grasp
my fingertips, feather the hair
against my temple
as it pulled me away?

Where did I go
when my eyes closed
in a rush to travel?
Heart thumped against my
chest, so loud the ancient drums
pressed down each foot fall

into the unspoiled soil.
Fire ablaze,
with flames almost as tall
as the tree limbs bowed down,
to twirl me in the dance
of my ancestors.

Until a spark
of sunlight scars my face.
I flinch under pressure,
my balance topples over boughs,
sets me adrift; my hands
grip sturdy bark.

Open eyes to blue sky,
home again,
I stand. Back against
the old fir;
gratitude for the many backs
who have stood before me.

I Live in the Rain

I live in the rain;
weeks and months of gray in my veins,
silver at the start, and then
reflecting
the rich glow of green—juniper and fir.

My gowns swell with waterfalls
dropping from ivory punchbowls;
celebration brims.
Vibrancy
dances atop rolling emerald hills.

Alas, too many days overcast my glow.
Hope drip-drops down swollen bones,
noisy splatter on concrete.
Saturated
colors drain to thunder and gloom.

Heavy hearts hide beneath wet soil,
patience tossed in the wind, until
that one sing-song morning,
glorious
golden rays of Spring casts her net—

And now I live in the sun,
blood rushing scarlet through my veins.

Forest, Golden Brown

Forest, golden brown,
rich in secrets,
for the quiet.

The still who stay
a short while
to view

are blessed
with her gifts.
For she welcomes

company who sees
with heart eyes
and hush lips.

Those who honor
her beauty
in browns so rich

they run deeper
than a river; blue,
wider than the open skies.

Russet and velvety,
chestnut, mahogany,
browns in faces

from history's past,
shining under layers
forgotten,

ignored, or worse,
in hopes
they disappear...

But the forest,
golden brown,
remembers

their names,
each and every soul,
like the stars

adorn her canopy,
waiting always
to be reflected.

Mango Moon

Long day melds
with an August sunset,
like seas on a still night.

Immovable slow breath,
relaxed and released
from the day's journey.

Heels hug sandy shores,
anchored heart sways,
now secure to drift—

to indulge in the offering;
pineapple juice drips
from coconut cocktails,

and mango moon
drops from a string
in the black sky—

bidding goodnight.

Shades of Sorrow

Soft shades of sorrow
blossomed
in arrangements sent.

They sat stoic,
unmoving
and picturesque

on the alter
prepared
for goodbye,

ingeniously
without scent
to carry home.

When hearts lament
there is no sound,
colors dim, and songs are still.

Poinsettia

Red star of Bethlehem
blooms in the seam of winter.
As legend goes, the same
"Flores de Noche Buena"
or
"Flowers of the Holy Night"
grow crimson
under Season's kiss.

Carried to the cross
by a little girl with empty hands;
nothing left to give
but the longing
of her tender heart.
And the night rejoiced,
while the Spirit danced
in Heaven's doorway.

Streamers flew from the sky,
painted lush leaves of green
in contrast.
Emptiness ran over
its brim; fulfilled.
Despair bled into divine-
gratification, while hope
leapt to the constellations above.

Poinsettia took its place
on a rocky roadside,
red star
shining miraculous—
forever remembrance
to walk in faith;
empty hands
are always full.

The Edge of Aging

Beauty walks in the night   sometimes
cloaked behind long withering days.

A season overspent, yet   unfinished,
desires a final word.

Pale eyes gleam beneath age   frailty
clings to bruised pear, ripened Mcintosh.

Thorny bones protrude, yet   connected,
tether stories to behold.

Earth's Honesty

Rain falls gray against the concrete,
reminders of Earth's renewal.
It takes time and patience,
neither of which I have
in this moment.

But the world grows around me,
unburdened by constant waiting,
while time slips in fairytale bubbles
behind my thoughts,
as if frozen.

And I take a breath—
a long slow inhale, seventy-eight
percent nitrogen, twenty percent oxygen,
argon, carbon dioxide—
though none of it

holds in my chest for very long. I gasp
clutching my coat, fall to my knees,
wet on the concrete. Cracks fill silver
reflections from the sky,
as it draws on truth:

Time doesn't wait for anyone,
anywhere, at any time, and I can't hate it
because it feels no remorse or sorrow.

Those are only emotions
projecting my own loss.

Renewal swirls with the rain,
silver-gray bleeds new colors like
oil rings on the road; rainbows without
eyes to see the tiny pots of gold
legend claims I'll find.

Instead I stand, accept the honesty;
realization cold with each icy drop.
The world never promised perfection.
In my life. In yours. The same rain falls
that fell thousands of years ago.

Like a machine doing its job.
The water cycle at its best. Sad songs sing,
but the Earth renews. Thunder cracks—
streaks the sky with light; witness
to another day sprouting green.

Stitching Left Behind

The sing-song sound
of spring
tugs a final thread
through my soul.

Loose stitching like
lavender
lies at my feet,
bare in the grass.

I step out, beyond
frayed edges,
worn skin slides
down my back,

falling to the earth
below,
tipped toes lose
tightened grip;

and I fly...

Gossamer Soul

Spun gold to gossamer,
beloved broken soul,
stretch your fingertips
to mine.

Fall into my wind
with each delicate
design,
hearts alight.

Let the sun rise,
ascend beyond
darkened sin,
past any shame.

Let truth wash clean
the cobwebs gathered,
withered now in dry grass,
healed from above.

These Hills (of Coastal Oregon)

Worn from the day
these hills,
with their round topped
blankets—gold and green,
lay quiet,
sun-drenched from summer.

Contrast to vibrant mornings,
these hills awaken
with fervor,
frantic and reaching
rays of splendor,
bursting wildflower blue.

Brimming in ardor,
these hills pulse,
their spirits dance,
roots curve and flow
under sky...then settle
down with setting sun—

alive and well fed.

Homecoming

The tenderness of a summer sky,
soft with breath, full of time.

Restful reminisce under indigo
wings, fall heavy with sleep.

Dreams come slow until they carry
weightless souls across the veil;

home.

White Blossoms

Winded
I look ahead to my daughter,
a younger
stronger version
of myself.

When did she grow
from vines of Sweet Autumn
Clematis
emitting stars
as she ascends.

I drink in her fragrance,
like a potion,
immortality
to lean on,
to breathe.

And I watch her inhale
a piece of sky,
a bite of courage
amongst tiny morsels
of self-awareness.

A keenness
that once stirred
in my womb.

Maybe even then
she knew who she would be—

Maybe even then
she felt her sun beams stretch
from fingertips
to tree limbs—

White blossoms in the wind.

The Color of Love

I wrap up in the color of you,
pure and translucent,
hazel eyes gleam in the moonlight.
Hidden hues hide
behind shadowed branches,
moss, and ivy
encircling our spot.

In the universe we stand
under the night sky,
your hand in mine,
walking in summer's warmth
left over
from the day we frolicked
through blades of grass.

We climbed the rocks,
admired the daisies,
spotted and few, but enough
to share in their purity,
not unlike your heart
that beats
against my chest.

When you cling to my side
golden locks lace the evening breeze,
tossing us back,

onto the blanket,
pink from your little girl room.
The place I never want you
far away, without stars to paint

your hands—ivory porcelain,
a pitcher never empty of giving.
Your arms, an eagle's wings
to fly home if ever
you are lost.
Your legs, sturdy as tall trunks
to hold up the sky...

And only because I love you
will I share you   with the earth.

About the Author

 Celaine Charles lives in the Pacific Northwest where she teaches, writes poetry and fiction, and blogs about her writing journey on her site, *Steps In Between*. The world around inspires her craft, and she thrives encouraging others to follow in their own creative paths. Her poetry series, *Colors*, launched June 2018 on *Channillo* and was awarded Best Continuing Series, Best New Series, and Best Poetry Series for the 2018 Channillo Awards. Previous works include shared poetry with the *Tupelo Press 30/30 Challenge Project*, and other publications: *Dime Show Review, Kingdoms in The Wild, Nature Writing, Nine Muses Poetry, Spillwords Press, The Seattle Star, The Sunlight Press,* and more. Author/DJ, Tamara Miles, has shared her poetry on SpiritPlants Radio, *Where the Light Most Falls*. In addition, Celaine was a poetry finalist in the *PNWA* (Pacific Northwest Writer's Association) Literary Contest, July 2017. *Colors Collected* is her first poetry book.

For more information, contact Celaine at the following links:

Email: celainecharles@gmail.com
Website: www.stepsinbetween.com
Channillo Series: https://channillo.com/series/colors/

You can also find Celaine on Facebook, Twitter, and Instagram.

Made in the USA
Monee, IL
24 November 2019